One Advance Against Arthr

(My recovery with the Margaret Hills' Diet)

When I stumbled down the organ-loft stairs and along the Church aisle to the communion rail, my knees swollen and my joints in agony, little did I realise how my life was going to change.

I had suffered with frequent bouts of bronchitis during the year and then my joints started to swell and become painful, each day a different one; classic 'flitting arthritis' my doctor called it.

In February 2005 my doctor diagnosed gout, blood tests were taken and I was prescribed anti-inflammatories and painkillers. The test results confirmed that I had arthritis. My health deteriorated and I was given stronger drugs. Then I carried a too-heavy supermarket basket and the next day I couldn't move out of bed and found myself in excruciating pain.

I had horrible sciatic pains up my left leg and it felt as if someone was drilling through the base of my spine. My doctor thought I'd slipped a disc, and arranged for an X-ray to be taken. Meanwhile I lay in bed, in agony, but had constantly to hobble to the bathroom with sickness and diarrhoea brought on by the ever-stronger drugs. My doctor told me that I obviously seemed to have a bad reaction to them, and that I should 'come off' all that he'd prescribed. I lost two stone in a week, the sciatic pains plagued me day and night and I couldn't sleep for weeks.

A kindly friend delivered a punnet of raspberries to cheer me up. The next day the pain was unbearable and I rang my doctor's surgery for help but was told that I'd been prescribed everything possible.

The X-ray revealed 'spondylosis' - arthritis at the base of my spine, and I was given a specialist's appointment, for which I had to wait a few weeks. In the end my recovery was so swift that I was able to cancel it.

My daughter, upset after a 'phone call to me, found a book on ebay and it arrived a couple of days later. She was hardly to know just how relevant and helpful this publication was to be.

It was called 'Curing Arthritis the Drug-free Way' and was written by Margaret Hills, SRN, who, as a young woman, had been crippled by rheumatoid and osteo arthritis. When orthodox treatment could do nothing for her, she used her nurse's training to develop her simple natural cure, which, against all her doctor's predictions, was completely successful! She later opened a clinic and wrote other books to help fellow sufferers.

After reading the book, I decided to follow the instructions, rolled out of bed and started to exercise my muscles and tottered up and down the garden, in agony, to try and get moving.

My husband and son drove me to our supermarket and, armed with my new shopping list, from the book, I filled my trolley with organic vegetables, non-citric organic fruits, unrefined sugar, molasses, olive spread instead of butter, wholemeal flour, wholemeal bread, cider-vinegar, organic honey and non-citric fruit juices. Whole-wheat pasta and wholegrain rice were put in with free-range organic chicken, lamb and turkey, as young meat has less uric acid in it. I finished off with fresh fish.

I would have to change to skimmed milk from my milkman and I had to avoid butter and cream. I was only allowed three eggs a week, no beef or pork, no chocolate or cocoa, nor a lot of fruits that contain Vitamin C - like oranges, grapefruit, plums, grapes, nectarines, any berries/juices and even tomatoes - this explained my reaction to the raspberries.

My son looked alarmed, 'We're not eating all that stuff are we?' My shopping had changed dramatically from the week before.

That night I demanded an Epsom-salt bath, as instructed in my new book! Epsom salts draw things out through the pores in your skin by ion exchange, apparently. 'Drawing ointment' is an old-fashioned remedy for boils, and is concentrated $MgSO_4$ (Epsom salts); my ever helpful husband produced a jar of this from his chemical collection in the garage and tipped the whole lot (500g) into the warm bathwater. I wallowed for fifteen minutes, dried off and snuggled down. I awoke refreshed - my first decent night's sleep since the onset of the arthritis flare-up - and showered. My hopes began to rise - this might be a miracle cure!

Apparently it's not a diet for life. Margaret Hills took one year to cure herself and it was permanent! Once you are really free of the disease (dis-ease) then you can introduce some favourite foods again. I was intrigued by a contact address at the back of the book and rang the Margaret Hills Clinic. I then decided to register with them and after receiving a detailed, tailored reply I ordered food supplements from them to make up for foods that I had to exclude.

The most difficult exclusion was the biscuits in my biscuit barrel. No longer could I just grab one and fill in a peckish moment. I had first to weigh out all ingredients and cook them from scratch. I even used fresh yeast and made my own bread.

The aim is to exclude all preservatives and additives normally found in processed foods. Lunch,for instance, might include a poached egg on homemade bread or a baked potato with lettuce and cottage cheese. I make soups using meatstock from the Sunday's roast or from vegetables. For a pudding I'll have a banana or apple and maybe a few homemade biscuits. I'm allowed apple juice, to drink - but not orange juice, of course! When out visiting, I'll go for the 'basic' choice on the menu; jacket potato with tuna and salad, perhaps, but avoiding the tomatoes.

Choosing organic vegetables and fruit excludes the possibility of pest-spray residues being left on them. Tea and coffee were forbidden as well. However, I did keep drinking them, but greatly diluted. In restaurants now, I'll ask for extra hot water and a spare cup, in order to dilute the 'brew' right down. To get the most nutrition from the foods one is allowed to eat, Margaret Hills recommends wholegrain, wholemeal everything. It all made sense. (The arthritis started to return if I deviated from my diet for even a few days, so for me anyway, it seems to be related). This was not a gimmicky diet but just good, wholesome, untainted food.

I ordered the 'Exercise' book and started walking around the block daily. Now, in 2009, I swim regularly as well. I take the exercise part of the regime very seriously and either go for a walk or swim first thing in the morning. It's something that's always on my mind, as it's so easy to slip back into old habits.

When I attended the physio session my doctor had ordered, the therapist told me that from the x-ray he could see that a few of the joints in my spine had seized up and when he tried manipulation, it only made things worse. So the next appointment was put on hold. In the end, I didn't need to return for another session.

Cider vinegar mixed with molasses (a gentle but very effective laxative) and honey was taken three times a day and last thing at night (always after some food). One teaspoon of molasses goes in a cup with a splash of boiling water (I use sugar molasses, but these are not as nutritious as the 'black-strap' molasses the clinic recommends.) Then I add a teaspoon of honey and two dessertspoons of organic cider-vinegar and sip it slowly.

Just make sure you're aware of the effect of them, and take this into account if you have to go out of the house!

The vitamin supplements ('Formula') and protein powder arrived from the clinic and I started to take them regularly as well - I buy the vegetarian form,as I find them much easier to take. Within one week my depression had lifted and I seemed to have more energy - for more exercise! After three weeks the sciatic pains started to go and three months later they had completely disappeared. My appointment with a specialist was cancelled, as it wasn't necessary any more!

Now, in 2009, I still stick to the diet, take the supplements and cider vinegar and have two or three Epsom salt baths a week. Occasionally I have an epsom foot bath, if my feet feel particularly achy. I put one cupful of epsom salts in a bowl of lovely warm water and soak my feet for fifteen minutes, dry them off and put socks on to keep them warm. Bliss!

Occasionally I suffer a flare-up, but it is only slight and goes within days. It usually occurs if I've been away for a few days and have had to eat processed foods, or if I've been under emotional stress.

I've never felt healthier, and even my occasional migraines have cleared up. A caller requesting my booklet suggested switching to Wholemeal Spelt Flour and I haven't suffered since. Apparently our digestive systems are more suited to this earlier form of wheat but modern varieties have been developed with a higher gluten content to suit the processed food industry. Anyway, the Margaret Hills' approach to arthritis and general health seems to have worked well for me, and I hope my experience can help other sufferers out there.

Overcoming problems with this approach

I was in so much pain that I immediately followed everything the book suggested as a desperate attempt to relieve my suffering - a bit of a shock to the system, as it all seemed so different from my normal routine. Having to make up the cider-vinegar mixture after every meal was strange, at first, and took some getting used to. The clinic advise you to dilute the mixture with water but I found it easier to 'down it', if there was only a small amount to drink. Now, I can't imagine not taking it regularly and would miss it !

When going out for the day, I always take doses with me, in small screw-top bottles. The first things packed for holidays are the ingredients I need to make up the concoction plus, of course, the vitamin supplements (formula), protein powder and some dried skimmed milk to help make up this mixture. Epsom salts for a bath are usually included as well, and we try to arrange to stay somewhere where a bath is available. The ingredients for the mixture can be obtained from any large supermarket or a health food shop, and the epsom salts from a chemist or garden centre (as Magnesium Sulphate).

Getting by without my previously frequent cups of tea and coffee was quite difficult, but they're very acidic. I think this was the biggest change in my attitude and I've noticed how people frequently drink such strong beverages. Now I only make a very weak brew and not very often. This is important!

The diet, itself, took some getting used to and I missed eating beef, pork, ham, deep fried fish and chips, strawberries, cream, butter and all the other lovely foods I'd happily eaten for years! Only recently have I been able to enjoy having some of these on special occasions without ill effects afterwards. Arthritis flare-ups have been much fewer and further between recently and I really feel more confident about my health. Still, when I'm at home I still stick to the diet and just throw caution to the wind when having an occasional meal out.

The Epsom salt baths are very therapeutic and as a result I suffer fewer migraines, feel calmer and any muscle aches or pains, from gardening or going for country walks, for instance, are soothed away overnight.

All in all my dramatic change of habits from my former life to the one I lead now has been a huge success and one I'll never regret. *Sarah Gall*

It might be wise to contact the Margaret Hills' Clinic if you think you'd like to try their approach, as they're able to take into consideration other health conditions, for example cancer, diabetes, high blood pressure or heart conditions, that you might be suffering from before giving you helpful advice. Anyone taking warfarin should definitely contact them before starting the diet.

Helpful Exercises

When I read the book by Margaret Hills, I realised that despite all my aches and pains, exercise could only improve things and would eventually help to relieve my suffering. This approach to treating arthritis is a 'self-help' one and makes you feel that you are more in control of your condition.

The clinic supplied me with a book of helpful exercises and together with other literature I soon found ones that really made a difference. They were all very gentle and I knew they couldn't do any harm. I'd go through my routine first thing in the morning and finish off with a walk around the block.

The following I found particularly helpful for my condition (arthritis in my spine and the subsequent sciatic pains). I would repeat each exercise five times.

1. <u>Back exercises</u>
Lying in bed, press spine down into the mattress, hold it there to the count of ten, and then release.

2. <u>Ankle exercise</u>
Rotate ankles so that your feet point in, hold, and then rotate them away from each other.

3. <u>Foot movements</u>
Move left foot round in a clockwise circle. Then the other way. Repeat with the other foot.

4. <u>Toe Exercise</u>
Curl toes tightly then straighten and spread them as far as possible.

5. <u>Stretching ankles</u>
Sit on a chair with both feet flat on the floor. Raise heels but keep toes on the floor. Put them down again and raise toes but keep heels on the floor.

6. Foot movements

Sitting in a chair, raise heels off the floor, swivel them to the right and down on to floor. Raise toes and arches, leaving heels on floor and swivel fronts of feet to the right. Repeat back to the left.

7. Rolling Pin exercise

Work a rolling- pin, on the floor, with feet.

8. A stretching exercise

With knees apart and feet flat on the floor, lift arches so only the outer edges of feet remain on floor. Then repeat, moving knees together so big toes and inner heels stay on floor.

9. Achilles Stretch.

With your hands on a wall at shoulder height and your feet a few inches from the base of the wall, extend left leg behind you, keeping left knee straight, toes on floor and left heel raised (right knee can be bent if necessary).
Try to lower left heel to floor, feeling stretch.
Repeat with right leg.

10. Walking exercise

Walk a few paces on tiptoe then a few paces on heels.

11. Strengthening ankles

Holding the back of a chair, rise up on tiptoe, then come down slowly. Next, raise toes so that you are standing on your heels and come down slowly again.

12. Toe Exercise

Sitting on a chair, pick up scattered marbles with toes.

13.Foot See-saw
Holding the back of a chair, raise left heel, leaving toes on floor. While lowering left heel, raise right heel. Repeat.

Recipe suggestions

Six of my favourite

I don't use any baking powder or raising agents, as these are acidic. To encourage cakes to rise, I try to whisk eggs as much as possible and fold in the flour carefully to prevent the gluten being released, as this can make the mixture sticky and heavy.

I always use wholemeal flour (if possible stoneground) and olive-oil spread instead of butter or margarine. Muscovado sugar (light or dark) is better than refined white sugar.

The cakes and biscuits are best eaten on the same or following day.

1. Lentil Soup
2½ pt meat or vegetable stock
1lb carrots
1 onion
1 leek
6 handfuls of red-split lentils
Seasoning

Heat up stock in pressure cooker
Add sliced onion, carrots, leek and add seasoning.
Add lentils.

Pressure cook for 20 minutes.
When de-pressurised use a blender to make mixture into soup.

2. Fish Pie
2½ lb potatoes
1 large fillet of fish
1lb carrots
1 oz olive spread
2oz wholemeal flour
½ pt skimmed milk
Seasoning
Handful of fresh parsley
1 leek

Boil or pressure cook potatoes and sliced carrots.
Steam fish in milk with sliced leek
Put olive spread in pan on low heat.
When melted, add flour and make into roux; add seasoning and mustard.
When fish is cooked, strain off milk and add, gradually, to roux to make sauce.
Chop up parsley and mix into sauce.
Put fish in bottom of pyrex dish, put carrots on top and then pour sauce on top.
Mash potatoes, with olive spread and seasoning, and put on top of fish and sauce.
Grill until golden brown.

3. Ginger Oat Biscuits
4oz olive oil spread
1 dessertspoonful of honey (instead of syrup)
3oz muscovado sugar

4oz wholemeal flour
4oz oats
1 tsp. ground ginger (optional)
A pinch of sea salt

Preheat oven to gas mark 3 (150 C, if fan assisted).
Gently heat olive spread, sugar and honey in small saucepan until all fat is dissolved.
Mix dry ingredients together and add to honey mixture.
Take smallish blobs, with a spoon, and place on tray. Form into balls and flatten with fork.
Bake for 10-15 mins
Transfer to wire tray. Store in airtight tin.

4. Wholemeal Oat Biscuits
6oz wholemeal flour
 a pinch of sea salt
6oz oats
6oz olive spread (instead of margarine or butter)
41/2 oz muscovado sugar
1 size 1 egg
1 dessertspoonful of honey (instead of syrup)

Pre-heat oven to gas mark 5 (170C if fan assisted).
Lightly grease a baking sheet.
(It's best if you can use an electric mixer).
Weigh out flour and add egg and honey mixed together. Add the rest of the ingredients to form a dough.
Roll out to ¼ inch thickness (not too thinly) and cut into rounds and place on baking sheet.
Bake for 10-15 mins.on a high shelf.
Transfer on to wire tray.
Store in airtight tin.

5. Ginger and Apple cake
4oz olive oil spread
8oz muscovado sugar
2 eggs
8oz wholemeal flour.
A pinch of sea salt
2 tsp ground ginger
10oz peeled diced cooking apples

Topping:
2 tsp honey
2 tsp muscovado sugar

Preheat oven to gas mark 3 (150C, if fan assisted).
Cream olive oil spread and sugar.
Add beaten eggs gradually.
Fold in flour, salt and ground ginger carefully and add apple.
Bake for 50 mins in centre of oven on a greased sandwich tin.
Spread topping while cake is still hot.

6. Victoria Sandwich.
Weigh 3 eggs
 Same weight of olive spread
Same weight of muscovado sugar
Same weight of wholemeal flour (no raising agent)
Pinch of sea salt
2 or 3 cooking apples, peeled, sliced, cooked with 1
dessertspoon of honey and muscovado sugar (to taste), and
puréed
(or you can use stewed apricots)

Cream olive spread and sugar.
Whisk eggs and add to mixture using a balloon whisk (to incorporate as much air as possible).
Add flour carefully and gently using a spoon.
Divide mixture between two greased sponge tins.
Bake on shelf above middle of oven at 180C for 10-15 mins.
When cooled on wire tray, spread each half of sandwich with puréed apple, or apricot, mixture.

Do it Soon Enough

My grandmother suffered badly with arthritis and my sister and I seem to have inherited a tendency towards this disease.

My sister is five years older than I am but has already had both hip joints replaced. She did try the Margaret Hills Diet when I started to recover from my illness, but sadly, by that time the arthritis had damaged her joints irreparably.

Actually, although she didn't mind drinking the cider-vinegar mixture she found it difficult to exclude some of her favourite foods from her diet. I think she grows a lot of soft-fruit in her garden and she couldn't bear to see it 'go to waste'!

As my arthritis flare-up was so severe and I suffered so badly with the pain, I was driven to extreme lengths and immediately followed the diet suggestions exactly. Consequently I was spared any joint damage as the cider-vinegar seems to 'get rid of' any arthritis in my body.

If

A much happier Sarah, photographed in April 2009 with husband and daughter, after following the diet

you would like to receive a copy of this book, please could you send a cheque for £3.50 (includes postage and packing), made payable to SDA Technical Publications:
SDA Technical Publications, Unit 30, Willan Industrial Estate, West Ashton Street, Eccles New Road, Salford, M50 2GR.
Tel:0161 745 7029   Fax:0161 745 9649
email:sarahgall@hotmail.co.uk   Tel: 01706 344429

Postscript, January 2010

Timescale of my recovery

17th February 2005: gout diagnosed in my knee.

24th February: blood test revealed arthritis.

17th June: severe flare-up in my spine. Friend gave me raspberries to cheer me up. Pain became unbearable. After reading Margaret Hills' book, realised why I reacted so badly to them. Changed diet, started taking cider vinegar, had first epsom bath.

15th July: able to walk, but not well enough to attend my son's graduation ceremony.

21st July: x ray confirmed arthritis.

25th July: started on Margaret Hills supplements (formula), protein and zinc.

3rd August: Visit to doctor for minor, unrelated matter. He was amazed at my improvement.

13th August: went on holiday.

24th August: cancelled specialist's appointment, as no need to attend.

28th August: returned to playing the organ for services at both churches.

I take the cider vinegar remedy four times a day: I put one teaspoon of runny honey in organic cider vinegar and dilute with 3rd pint cold water. I take it after each meal, after food and before bed (so 4 times a day). I also take a teaspoon of black-strap molasses three times a day (or, equally effective, 1 alfalfa capsule three times a day - from M.H. Clinic). You can buy organic cider vinegar and molasses in health food shops. I use local or raw unpasteurised honey from supermarkets.

Epsom salts (magnesium sulphate) can be bought from chemists - and garden centres (!)

If you're diabetic or on warfarin, it's best to contact the Margaret Hills Clinic - they'll adapt the diet/remedy for you (see booklet for contact details.)

From my experience the quickest way to a pain-free life is to exercise, take the cider vinegar doses regularly, try to <u>avoid</u> alcohol, reduce sugar/foods containing sugar, processed foods, avoid beef, pork, butter, cheese and full-cream milk, tomatoes, citrus fruits, grapes, pineapples, grapefruit, chocolate, any berries or their juices, rhubarb, drink extremely weak tea or coffee, if at all and take regular epsom salt baths, if your health permits you to (see booklet) and avoid stress.

These are the foods that I eat, on the diet: fish, chicken, turkey, lamb, eggs, skimmed milk, olive spread, cottage cheese, home-made whole wheat bread, tea, coffee (both very dilute), apple juice, unsalted nuts, wholegrain rice, wholemeal spaghetti, oats, Weetabix, Shredded Wheat, potatoes, all vegetables (apart from tomatoes), pulses (except 'baked beans' in tomato sauce!), mushrooms, salad ingredients (no tomatoes), apples, pears, bananas, apricots, melon (but no berries or berry juices). Dried apricots (not raisins, sultanas, currants, dates, figs or prunes), wholemeal flour, organic cider vinegar, honey, black-strap molasses, apricot jam (if no citric acid).

Many people have been in touch to report their success (see separate sheet). If no improvement, contact the clinic - your condition may be more complex than you think.

I have to admit a setback just after New Year. For a few months previously I'd been reverting to old habits and using self-raising flour, cocoa and coffee to make cakes. Over Christmas I'd treated myself to eating chocolate and also sausage, ham and bacon. On 1st January my feet flared up and then my ankles swelled. The Clinic suggested that I went back to my strict diet, changed to using organic cider vinegar with Mother liquor and cut out all foods with added sugar (so no cakes or biscuits). I bathed my feet and ankles in buckets of warm water with a cupful of epsom salts in and had full epsom baths every other day. After a week, the problem had virtually gone.

Over 450 people have contacted me since the recent Daily Mail and Daily Express articles about the booklet that I've written about my recovery from arthritis.

Among them are seven who have started to feel a noticeable improvement in their condition after just one week on the cider vinegar remedy and avoiding certain foods. They are:

1. A lady who emailed me to say that even just bathing her hands in a warm solution of Epsom salts was helping her.

2. A gentleman from Northern Ireland was pleased that his 'golfing' hand was less stiff and painful.

3. A woman from Northern Ireland (unrelated) rang to say that her ankle felt so much better.

4. A man from Birmingham rang to say that his shoulder felt much better. He was looking forward to buying a dog, as he felt he could now take it for walks.

5. A woman rang me from Birmingham, requesting the Margaret Hills book, as well (I have a few to sell at home), as her shoulder was far less painful and she believed that the remedy was working and she wanted to read up more about it.

6. A lady I met where I go swimming said her husband's neck was much better now, after trying the remedy.

7. A midwife who rang from the West Midlands was amazed how quickly she started to feel better. She rang me after a week on the remedy/diet.

They all said they'd write to me in a month or so when they felt their condition had really started to clear up properly.

These are among several people who've contacted me with improvements since my booklet was published last July. Over 2000 copies have been sold.

I'm happy to try to answer any questions and I would be really interested to hear how you progress.